Hi,

My name is Ima and I'm a gnome. I created this book for you to keep track of all the important details as you bring more friends of mine to life.

What's your name? ____

Additional notes:

Selfie

Date I was created: ______________________________

How tall I am: __________ My colors: ______________________

Theme or holiday: ______________________________

The name my human gave me: ______________________

Materials Used to Make Me	Bought From	Price
Hat/hair:		
Body:		
Nose:		
Beard:		
Arms/legs:		
Shoes:		
Filling/stuffing:		
Other:		
Embellishments:		
Accessories:		

Difficulty level: Easy ① ② ③ ④ ⑤ Hard

Was I commissioned? Yes ○ No ○

My ultimate destiny: Kept ○ Gifted ○ Sold ○

Cost to make me: __________

If gifted or sold, person received: ______________________

If sold, price and date: ______________________

Additional notes:

Selfie

Date I was created: ______________________________

How tall I am: __________ My colors: ______________________

Theme or holiday: ______________________________

The name my human gave me: ______________________________

Materials Used to Make Me	Bought From	Price
Hat/hair:		
Body:		
Nose:		
Beard:		
Arms/legs:		
Shoes:		
Filling/stuffing:		
Other:		
Embellishments:		
Accessories:		

Difficulty level: Easy ① ② ③ ④ ⑤ Hard

Was I commissioned? Yes ○ No ○

My ultimate destiny: Kept ○ Gifted ○ Sold ○

Cost to make me: __________

If gifted or sold, person received: ______________________________

If sold, price and date: ______________________________

Additional notes:

Selfie

Date I was created: ____________________

How tall I am: __________ My colors: ____________________

Theme or holiday: ____________________

The name my human gave me: ____________________

Materials Used to Make Me	Bought From	Price
Hat/hair:		
Body:		
Nose:		
Beard:		
Arms/legs:		
Shoes:		
Filling/stuffing:		
Other:		
Embellishments:		
Accessories:		

Difficulty level: Easy ① ② ③ ④ ⑤ Hard

Was I commissioned? Yes ○ No ○

My ultimate destiny: Kept ○ Gifted ○ Sold ○

Cost to make me: __________

If gifted or sold, person received: ____________________

If sold, price and date: ____________________

Additional notes:

Selfie

Date I was created: ______________________________

How tall I am: __________ My colors: ______________________

Theme or holiday: ______________________________

The name my human gave me: ______________________________

Materials Used to Make Me	Bought From	Price
Hat/hair:		
Body:		
Nose:		
Beard:		
Arms/legs:		
Shoes:		
Filling/stuffing:		
Other:		
Embellishments:		
Accessories:		

Difficulty level: Easy ① ② ③ ④ ⑤ Hard

Was I commissioned? Yes ○ No ○

My ultimate destiny: Kept ○ Gifted ○ Sold ○

Cost to make me: __________

If gifted or sold, person received: ______________________________

If sold, price and date: ______________________________

Additional notes: ____

Selfie

Date I was created: ______________________________

How tall I am: __________ My colors: ____________________

Theme or holiday: ______________________________

The name my human gave me: ______________________________

Materials Used to Make Me	Bought From	Price
Hat/hair:		
Body:		
Nose:		
Beard:		
Arms/legs:		
Shoes:		
Filling/stuffing:		
Other:		
Embellishments:		
Accessories:		

Difficulty level: Easy ① ② ③ ④ ⑤ Hard

Was I commissioned? Yes ○ No ○

My ultimate destiny: Kept ○ Gifted ○ Sold ○

Cost to make me: __________

If gifted or sold, person received: ______________________________

If sold, price and date: ______________________________

Additional notes:

Selfie

Date I was created: ______________________________

How tall I am: __________ My colors: ______________________

Theme or holiday: ______________________________

The name my human gave me: ______________________________

Materials Used to Make Me	Bought From	Price
Hat/hair:		
Body:		
Nose:		
Beard:		
Arms/legs:		
Shoes:		
Filling/stuffing:		
Other:		
Embellishments:		
Accessories:		

Difficulty level: (Easy) ① ② ③ ④ ⑤ (Hard)

Was I commissioned? Yes ○ No ○

My ultimate destiny: Kept ○ Gifted ○ Sold ○

Cost to make me: __________

If gifted or sold, person received: ______________________________

If sold, price and date: ______________________________

Additional notes:

Selfie

Date I was created: ______________________

How tall I am: __________ My colors: ______________

Theme or holiday: ______________________

The name my human gave me: ______________________

Materials Used to Make Me	Bought From	Price
Hat/hair:		
Body:		
Nose:		
Beard:		
Arms/legs:		
Shoes:		
Filling/stuffing:		
Other:		
Embellishments:		
Accessories:		

Difficulty level: Easy ① ② ③ ④ ⑤ Hard

Was I commissioned? Yes ○ No ○

My ultimate destiny: Kept ○ Gifted ○ Sold ○

Cost to make me: __________

If gifted or sold, person received: ______________________

If sold, price and date: ______________________

Additional notes:

Selfie

Date I was created: ______________________________

How tall I am: __________ My colors: ______________________

Theme or holiday: ______________________________

The name my human gave me: ______________________________

Materials Used to Make Me	Bought From	Price
Hat/hair:		
Body:		
Nose:		
Beard:		
Arms/legs:		
Shoes:		
Filling/stuffing:		
Other:		
Embellishments:		
Accessories:		

Difficulty level: Easy ① ② ③ ④ ⑤ Hard

Was I commissioned? Yes ○ No ○

My ultimate destiny: Kept ○ Gifted ○ Sold ○

Cost to make me: __________

If gifted or sold, person received: ______________________________

If sold, price and date: ______________________________

Additional notes: ________________________________

Selfie

Date I was created: ________________________________

How tall I am: __________ My colors: ________________

Theme or holiday: ________________________________

The name my human gave me: ________________________

Materials Used to Make Me	Bought From	Price
Hat/hair:		
Body:		
Nose:		
Beard:		
Arms/legs:		
Shoes:		
Filling/stuffing:		
Other:		
Embellishments:		
Accessories:		

Difficulty level: Easy ① ② ③ ④ ⑤ Hard

Was I commissioned? Yes ○ No ○

My ultimate destiny: Kept ○ Gifted ○ Sold ○

Cost to make me: __________

If gifted or sold, person received: ____________________

If sold, price and date: ____________________________

Additional notes:

Selfie

Date I was created: ______________________________

How tall I am: __________ My colors: ______________________

Theme or holiday: ______________________________

The name my human gave me: ______________________________

Materials Used to Make Me	Bought From	Price
Hat/hair:		
Body:		
Nose:		
Beard:		
Arms/legs:		
Shoes:		
Filling/stuffing:		
Other:		
Embellishments:		
Accessories:		

Difficulty level: (Easy) ① ② ③ ④ ⑤ (Hard)

Was I commissioned? Yes ○ No ○

My ultimate destiny: Kept ○ Gifted ○ Sold ○

Cost to make me: __________

If gifted or sold, person received: ______________________________

If sold, price and date: ______________________________

Additional notes:

Selfie

Date I was created: ______________________________

How tall I am: __________ My colors: ______________________

Theme or holiday: ______________________________

The name my human gave me: ______________________________

Materials Used to Make Me	Bought From	Price
Hat/hair:		
Body:		
Nose:		
Beard:		
Arms/legs:		
Shoes:		
Filling/stuffing:		
Other:		
Embellishments:		
Accessories:		

Difficulty level: Easy ① ② ③ ④ ⑤ Hard

Was I commissioned? Yes ○ No ○

My ultimate destiny: Kept ○ Gifted ○ Sold ○

Cost to make me: __________

If gifted or sold, person received: ______________________________

If sold, price and date: ______________________________

Additional notes: ____________________

Selfie

Date I was created: ______________________________

How tall I am: __________ My colors: ______________________

Theme or holiday: ______________________________

The name my human gave me: ______________________

Materials Used to Make Me	Bought From	Price
Hat/hair:		
Body:		
Nose:		
Beard:		
Arms/legs:		
Shoes:		
Filling/stuffing:		
Other:		
Embellishments:		
Accessories:		

Difficulty level: Easy ① ② ③ ④ ⑤ Hard

Was I commissioned? Yes ○ No ○

My ultimate destiny: Kept ○ Gifted ○ Sold ○

Cost to make me: __________

If gifted or sold, person received: ______________________

If sold, price and date: ______________________

Additional notes:

Selfie

Date I was created: ____

How tall I am: __________ My colors: ____________________________

Theme or holiday: ____

The name my human gave me: ______________________________

Materials Used to Make Me	Bought From	Price
Hat/hair:		
Body:		
Nose:		
Beard:		
Arms/legs:		
Shoes:		
Filling/stuffing:		
Other:		
Embellishments:		
Accessories:		

Difficulty level: Easy ① ② ③ ④ ⑤ Hard

Was I commissioned? Yes ○ No ○

My ultimate destiny: Kept ○ Gifted ○ Sold ○

Cost to make me: __________

If gifted or sold, person received: ______________________________

If sold, price and date: ____

Additional notes:

Selfie

Date I was created: ______________________________

How tall I am: __________ My colors: ______________________

Theme or holiday: ______________________________

The name my human gave me: ______________________________

Materials Used to Make Me	Bought From	Price
Hat/hair:		
Body:		
Nose:		
Beard:		
Arms/legs:		
Shoes:		
Filling/stuffing:		
Other:		
Embellishments:		
Accessories:		

Difficulty level: Easy ① ② ③ ④ ⑤ Hard

Was I commissioned? Yes ○ No ○

My ultimate destiny: Kept ○ Gifted ○ Sold ○

Cost to make me: __________

If gifted or sold, person received: ______________________________

If sold, price and date: ______________________________

Additional notes:

Selfie

Date I was created: ______________________________

How tall I am: ____________ My colors: ______________________

Theme or holiday: ______________________________

The name my human gave me: ______________________

Materials Used to Make Me	Bought From	Price
Hat/hair:		
Body:		
Nose:		
Beard:		
Arms/legs:		
Shoes:		
Filling/stuffing:		
Other:		
Embellishments:		
Accessories:		

Difficulty level: Easy ① ② ③ ④ ⑤ Hard

Was I commissioned? Yes ○ No ○

My ultimate destiny: Kept ○ Gifted ○ Sold ○

Cost to make me: ____________

If gifted or sold, person received: ______________________

If sold, price and date: ______________________

Additional notes:

Selfie

Date I was created: ____________________

How tall I am: __________ My colors: ____________________

Theme or holiday: ____________________

The name my human gave me: ____________________

Materials Used to Make Me	Bought From	Price
Hat/hair:		
Body:		
Nose:		
Beard:		
Arms/legs:		
Shoes:		
Filling/stuffing:		
Other:		
Embellishments:		
Accessories:		

Difficulty level: Easy ① ② ③ ④ ⑤ Hard

Was I commissioned? Yes ○ No ○

My ultimate destiny: Kept ○ Gifted ○ Sold ○

Cost to make me: __________

If gifted or sold, person received: ____________________

If sold, price and date: ____________________

Additional notes:

Selfie

Date I was created: ____________________

How tall I am: __________ My colors: ____________________

Theme or holiday: ____________________

The name my human gave me: ____________________

Materials Used to Make Me	Bought From	Price
Hat/hair:		
Body:		
Nose:		
Beard:		
Arms/legs:		
Shoes:		
Filling/stuffing:		
Other:		
Embellishments:		
Accessories:		

Difficulty level: Easy ① ② ③ ④ ⑤ Hard

Was I commissioned? Yes ○ No ○

My ultimate destiny: Kept ○ Gifted ○ Sold ○

Cost to make me: __________

If gifted or sold, person received: ____________________

If sold, price and date: ____________________

Additional notes:

Selfie

Date I was created: ______________________________

How tall I am: __________ My colors: ______________________

Theme or holiday: ______________________________

The name my human gave me: ______________________________

Materials Used to Make Me	Bought From	Price
Hat/hair:		
Body:		
Nose:		
Beard:		
Arms/legs:		
Shoes:		
Filling/stuffing:		
Other:		
Embellishments:		
Accessories:		

Difficulty level: (Easy) ① ② ③ ④ ⑤ (Hard)

Was I commissioned? Yes ○ No ○

My ultimate destiny: Kept ○ Gifted ○ Sold ○

Cost to make me: __________

If gifted or sold, person received: ______________________________

If sold, price and date: ______________________________

Additional notes:

Selfie

Date I was created: ______________________________

How tall I am: __________ My colors: ______________________

Theme or holiday: ______________________________

The name my human gave me: ______________________________

Materials Used to Make Me	Bought From	Price
Hat/hair:		
Body:		
Nose:		
Beard:		
Arms/legs:		
Shoes:		
Filling/stuffing:		
Other:		
Embellishments:		
Accessories:		

Difficulty level: Easy ① ② ③ ④ ⑤ Hard

Was I commissioned? Yes ○ No ○

My ultimate destiny: Kept ○ Gifted ○ Sold ○

Cost to make me: __________

If gifted or sold, person received: ______________________________

If sold, price and date: ______________________________

Additional notes:

Selfie

Date I was created: ______________________________

How tall I am: __________ My colors: ______________________

Theme or holiday: ______________________________

The name my human gave me: ______________________________

Materials Used to Make Me	Bought From	Price
Hat/hair:		
Body:		
Nose:		
Beard:		
Arms/legs:		
Shoes:		
Filling/stuffing:		
Other:		
Embellishments:		
Accessories:		

Difficulty level: Easy ① ② ③ ④ ⑤ Hard

Was I commissioned? Yes ○ No ○

My ultimate destiny: Kept ○ Gifted ○ Sold ○

Cost to make me: __________

If gifted or sold, person received: ______________________________

If sold, price and date: ______________________________

Additional notes:

Selfie

Date I was created: ______________________________

How tall I am: __________ My colors: ______________________

Theme or holiday: ______________________________

The name my human gave me: ______________________________

Materials Used to Make Me	Bought From	Price
Hat/hair:		
Body:		
Nose:		
Beard:		
Arms/legs:		
Shoes:		
Filling/stuffing:		
Other:		
Embellishments:		
Accessories:		

Difficulty level: Easy ① ② ③ ④ ⑤ Hard

Was I commissioned? Yes ○ No ○

My ultimate destiny: Kept ○ Gifted ○ Sold ○

Cost to make me: __________

If gifted or sold, person received: ______________________________

If sold, price and date: ______________________________

Additional notes:

Selfie

Date I was created: ______________________________

How tall I am: __________ My colors: ______________________

Theme or holiday: ______________________________

The name my human gave me: ______________________________

Materials Used to Make Me	Bought From	Price
Hat/hair:		
Body:		
Nose:		
Beard:		
Arms/legs:		
Shoes:		
Filling/stuffing:		
Other:		
Embellishments:		
Accessories:		

Difficulty level: Easy ① ② ③ ④ ⑤ Hard

Was I commissioned? Yes ○ No ○

My ultimate destiny: Kept ○ Gifted ○ Sold ○

Cost to make me: __________

If gifted or sold, person received: ______________________________

If sold, price and date: ______________________________

Additional notes:

Selfie

Date I was created: ____________________

How tall I am: __________ My colors: ____________________

Theme or holiday: ____________________

The name my human gave me: ____________________

Materials Used to Make Me	Bought From	Price
Hat/hair:		
Body:		
Nose:		
Beard:		
Arms/legs:		
Shoes:		
Filling/stuffing:		
Other:		
Embellishments:		
Accessories:		

Difficulty level: Easy ① ② ③ ④ ⑤ Hard

Was I commissioned? Yes ○ No ○

My ultimate destiny: Kept ○ Gifted ○ Sold ○

Cost to make me: __________

If gifted or sold, person received: ____________________

If sold, price and date: ____________________

Additional notes:

Selfie

Date I was created: ______________________________

How tall I am: __________ My colors: ______________________

Theme or holiday: ______________________________

The name my human gave me: ______________________

Materials Used to Make Me	Bought From	Price
Hat/hair:		
Body:		
Nose:		
Beard:		
Arms/legs:		
Shoes:		
Filling/stuffing:		
Other:		
Embellishments:		
Accessories:		

Difficulty level: Easy ① ② ③ ④ ⑤ Hard

Was I commissioned? Yes ○ No ○

My ultimate destiny: Kept ○ Gifted ○ Sold ○

Cost to make me: __________

If gifted or sold, person received: ______________________

If sold, price and date: ______________________

Additional notes:

Selfie

Date I was created: ______________________________

How tall I am: __________ My colors: ______________________

Theme or holiday: ______________________________

The name my human gave me: ______________________

Materials Used to Make Me	Bought From	Price
Hat/hair:		
Body:		
Nose:		
Beard:		
Arms/legs:		
Shoes:		
Filling/stuffing:		
Other:		
Embellishments:		
Accessories:		

Difficulty level: Easy ① ② ③ ④ ⑤ Hard

Was I commissioned? Yes ○ No ○

My ultimate destiny: Kept ○ Gifted ○ Sold ○

Cost to make me: __________

If gifted or sold, person received: ______________________

If sold, price and date: ______________________________

Additional notes:

Selfie

Date I was created: ______________________________

How tall I am: __________ My colors: ______________________

Theme or holiday: ______________________________

The name my human gave me: ______________________

Materials Used to Make Me	Bought From	Price
Hat/hair:		
Body:		
Nose:		
Beard:		
Arms/legs:		
Shoes:		
Filling/stuffing:		
Other:		
Embellishments:		
Accessories:		

Difficulty level: (Easy) ① ② ③ ④ ⑤ (Hard)

Was I commissioned? Yes ○ No ○

My ultimate destiny: Kept ○ Gifted ○ Sold ○

Cost to make me: __________

If gifted or sold, person received: ______________________

If sold, price and date: ______________________

Additional notes:

Selfie

Date I was created: ______________________________

How tall I am: __________ My colors: ______________________

Theme or holiday: ______________________________

The name my human gave me: ______________________________

Materials Used to Make Me	Bought From	Price
Hat/hair:		
Body:		
Nose:		
Beard:		
Arms/legs:		
Shoes:		
Filling/stuffing:		
Other:		
Embellishments:		
Accessories:		

Difficulty level: Easy ① ② ③ ④ ⑤ Hard

Was I commissioned? Yes ○ No ○

My ultimate destiny: Kept ○ Gifted ○ Sold ○

Cost to make me: __________

If gifted or sold, person received: ______________________________

If sold, price and date: ______________________________

Additional notes:

Selfie

Date I was created: ______________________________

How tall I am: __________ My colors: ______________________

Theme or holiday: ______________________________

The name my human gave me: ______________________________

Materials Used to Make Me	Bought From	Price
Hat/hair:		
Body:		
Nose:		
Beard:		
Arms/legs:		
Shoes:		
Filling/stuffing:		
Other:		
Embellishments:		
Accessories:		

Difficulty level: Easy ① ② ③ ④ ⑤ Hard

Was I commissioned? Yes ○ No ○

My ultimate destiny: Kept ○ Gifted ○ Sold ○

Cost to make me: __________

If gifted or sold, person received: ______________________________

If sold, price and date: ______________________________

Additional notes:

Selfie

Date I was created: ____________________

How tall I am: __________ My colors: ____________________

Theme or holiday: ____________________

The name my human gave me: ____________________

Materials Used to Make Me	Bought From	Price
Hat/hair:		
Body:		
Nose:		
Beard:		
Arms/legs:		
Shoes:		
Filling/stuffing:		
Other:		
Embellishments:		
Accessories:		

Difficulty level: Easy ① ② ③ ④ ⑤ Hard

Was I commissioned? Yes ○ No ○

My ultimate destiny: Kept ○ Gifted ○ Sold ○

Cost to make me: __________

If gifted or sold, person received: ____________________

If sold, price and date: ____________________

Additional notes:

Selfie

Date I was created: ______________________________

How tall I am: ____________ My colors: ______________________

Theme or holiday: ______________________________

The name my human gave me: ______________________________

Materials Used to Make Me	Bought From	Price
Hat/hair:		
Body:		
Nose:		
Beard:		
Arms/legs:		
Shoes:		
Filling/stuffing:		
Other:		
Embellishments:		
Accessories:		

Difficulty level: Easy ① ② ③ ④ ⑤ Hard

Was I commissioned? Yes ○ No ○

My ultimate destiny: Kept ○ Gifted ○ Sold ○

Cost to make me: ____________

If gifted or sold, person received: ______________________________

If sold, price and date: ______________________________

Additional notes:

Selfie

Date I was created: ______________________________

How tall I am: __________ My colors: ______________________

Theme or holiday: ______________________________

The name my human gave me: ______________________________

Materials Used to Make Me	Bought From	Price
Hat/hair:		
Body:		
Nose:		
Beard:		
Arms/legs:		
Shoes:		
Filling/stuffing:		
Other:		
Embellishments:		
Accessories:		

Difficulty level: Easy ① ② ③ ④ ⑤ Hard

Was I commissioned? Yes ○ No ○

My ultimate destiny: Kept ○ Gifted ○ Sold ○

Cost to make me: __________

If gifted or sold, person received: ______________________________

If sold, price and date: ______________________________

Additional notes:

Selfie

Date I was created: ______________________________

How tall I am: __________ My colors: ______________________

Theme or holiday: ______________________________

The name my human gave me: ______________________________

Materials Used to Make Me	Bought From	Price
Hat/hair:		
Body:		
Nose:		
Beard:		
Arms/legs:		
Shoes:		
Filling/stuffing:		
Other:		
Embellishments:		
Accessories:		

Difficulty level: Easy ① ② ③ ④ ⑤ Hard

Was I commissioned? Yes ○ No ○

My ultimate destiny: Kept ○ Gifted ○ Sold ○

Cost to make me: __________

If gifted or sold, person received: ______________________________

If sold, price and date: ______________________________

Additional notes:

Selfie

Date I was created: ____________________

How tall I am: __________ My colors: ____________________

Theme or holiday: ____________________

The name my human gave me: ____________________

Materials Used to Make Me	Bought From	Price
Hat/hair:		
Body:		
Nose:		
Beard:		
Arms/legs:		
Shoes:		
Filling/stuffing:		
Other:		
Embellishments:		
Accessories:		

Difficulty level: Easy ① ② ③ ④ ⑤ Hard

Was I commissioned? Yes ○ No ○

My ultimate destiny: Kept ○ Gifted ○ Sold ○

Cost to make me: __________

If gifted or sold, person received: ____________________

If sold, price and date: ____________________

Additional notes:

Selfie

Date I was created: ______________________________

How tall I am: __________ My colors: ______________________

Theme or holiday: ______________________________

The name my human gave me: ______________________

Materials Used to Make Me	Bought From	Price
Hat/hair:		
Body:		
Nose:		
Beard:		
Arms/legs:		
Shoes:		
Filling/stuffing:		
Other:		
Embellishments:		
Accessories:		

Difficulty level: Easy ① ② ③ ④ ⑤ Hard

Was I commissioned? Yes ○ No ○

My ultimate destiny: Kept ○ Gifted ○ Sold ○

Cost to make me: __________

If gifted or sold, person received: ______________________

If sold, price and date: ______________________

Additional notes:

Selfie

Date I was created: ____________________

How tall I am: __________ My colors: ____________________

Theme or holiday: ____________________

The name my human gave me: ____________________

Materials Used to Make Me	Bought From	Price
Hat/hair:		
Body:		
Nose:		
Beard:		
Arms/legs:		
Shoes:		
Filling/stuffing:		
Other:		
Embellishments:		
Accessories:		

Difficulty level: Easy ① ② ③ ④ ⑤ Hard

Was I commissioned? Yes ○ No ○

My ultimate destiny: Kept ○ Gifted ○ Sold ○

Cost to make me: __________

If gifted or sold, person received: ____________________

If sold, price and date: ____________________

Additional notes:

Selfie

Date I was created: ___________________________

How tall I am: __________ My colors: ______________

Theme or holiday: ___________________________

The name my human gave me: ___________________

Materials Used to Make Me	Bought From	Price
Hat/hair:		
Body:		
Nose:		
Beard:		
Arms/legs:		
Shoes:		
Filling/stuffing:		
Other:		
Embellishments:		
Accessories:		

Difficulty level: Easy ① ② ③ ④ ⑤ Hard

Was I commissioned? Yes ○ No ○

My ultimate destiny: Kept ○ Gifted ○ Sold ○

Cost to make me: __________

If gifted or sold, person received: ___________________

If sold, price and date: ___________________

Additional notes:

Selfie

Date I was created: ______________________________

How tall I am: __________ My colors: ____________________

Theme or holiday: ______________________________

The name my human gave me: ______________________________

Materials Used to Make Me	Bought From	Price
Hat/hair:		
Body:		
Nose:		
Beard:		
Arms/legs:		
Shoes:		
Filling/stuffing:		
Other:		
Embellishments:		
Accessories:		

Difficulty level: Easy ① ② ③ ④ ⑤ Hard

Was I commissioned? Yes ○ No ○

My ultimate destiny: Kept ○ Gifted ○ Sold ○

Cost to make me: __________

If gifted or sold, person received: ______________________________

If sold, price and date: ______________________________

Additional notes:

Selfie

Date I was created: ______________________________

How tall I am: __________ My colors: ______________________

Theme or holiday: ______________________________

The name my human gave me: ______________________________

Materials Used to Make Me	Bought From	Price
Hat/hair:		
Body:		
Nose:		
Beard:		
Arms/legs:		
Shoes:		
Filling/stuffing:		
Other:		
Embellishments:		
Accessories:		

Difficulty level: Easy ① ② ③ ④ ⑤ Hard

Was I commissioned? Yes ○ No ○

My ultimate destiny: Kept ○ Gifted ○ Sold ○

Cost to make me: __________

If gifted or sold, person received: ______________________________

If sold, price and date: ______________________________

Additional notes:

Selfie

Date I was created: ______________________________

How tall I am: __________ My colors: ______________________

Theme or holiday: ______________________________

The name my human gave me: ______________________

Materials Used to Make Me	Bought From	Price
Hat/hair:		
Body:		
Nose:		
Beard:		
Arms/legs:		
Shoes:		
Filling/stuffing:		
Other:		
Embellishments:		
Accessories:		

Difficulty level: Easy ① ② ③ ④ ⑤ Hard

Was I commissioned? Yes ○ No ○

My ultimate destiny: Kept ○ Gifted ○ Sold ○

Cost to make me: __________

If gifted or sold, person received: ______________________

If sold, price and date: ______________________

Additional notes:

Selfie

Date I was created: ______________________________

How tall I am: __________ My colors: ______________________

Theme or holiday: ______________________________

The name my human gave me: ______________________________

Materials Used to Make Me	Bought From	Price
Hat/hair:		
Body:		
Nose:		
Beard:		
Arms/legs:		
Shoes:		
Filling/stuffing:		
Other:		
Embellishments:		
Accessories:		

Difficulty level: Easy ① ② ③ ④ ⑤ Hard

Was I commissioned? Yes ○ No ○

My ultimate destiny: Kept ○ Gifted ○ Sold ○

Cost to make me: __________

If gifted or sold, person received: ______________________________

If sold, price and date: ______________________________

Additional notes:

Selfie

Date I was created: ______________________________

How tall I am: __________ My colors: ______________________

Theme or holiday: ______________________________

The name my human gave me: ______________________________

Materials Used to Make Me	Bought From	Price
Hat/hair:		
Body:		
Nose:		
Beard:		
Arms/legs:		
Shoes:		
Filling/stuffing:		
Other:		
Embellishments:		
Accessories:		

Difficulty level: Easy ① ② ③ ④ ⑤ Hard

Was I commissioned? Yes ○ No ○

My ultimate destiny: Kept ○ Gifted ○ Sold ○

Cost to make me: __________

If gifted or sold, person received: ______________________________

If sold, price and date: ______________________________

Additional notes:

Selfie

Date I was created: ______________________________

How tall I am: __________ My colors: ______________________

Theme or holiday: ______________________________

The name my human gave me: ______________________

Materials Used to Make Me	Bought From	Price
Hat/hair:		
Body:		
Nose:		
Beard:		
Arms/legs:		
Shoes:		
Filling/stuffing:		
Other:		
Embellishments:		
Accessories:		

Difficulty level: Easy ① ② ③ ④ ⑤ Hard

Was I commissioned? Yes ○ No ○

My ultimate destiny: Kept ○ Gifted ○ Sold ○

Cost to make me: __________

If gifted or sold, person received: ______________________

If sold, price and date: ______________________

Additional notes:

Selfie

Date I was created: ____________________

How tall I am: __________ My colors: ____________________

Theme or holiday: ____________________

The name my human gave me: ____________________

Materials Used to Make Me	Bought From	Price
Hat/hair:		
Body:		
Nose:		
Beard:		
Arms/legs:		
Shoes:		
Filling/stuffing:		
Other:		
Embellishments:		
Accessories:		

Difficulty level: Easy ① ② ③ ④ ⑤ Hard

Was I commissioned? Yes ○ No ○

My ultimate destiny: Kept ○ Gifted ○ Sold ○

Cost to make me: __________

If gifted or sold, person received: ____________________

If sold, price and date: ____________________

Additional notes:

Selfie

Date I was created: ______________________________

How tall I am: __________ My colors: ______________________________

Theme or holiday: ______________________________

The name my human gave me: ______________________________

Materials Used to Make Me	Bought From	Price
Hat/hair:		
Body:		
Nose:		
Beard:		
Arms/legs:		
Shoes:		
Filling/stuffing:		
Other:		
Embellishments:		
Accessories:		

Difficulty level: Easy ① ② ③ ④ ⑤ Hard

Was I commissioned? Yes ○ No ○

My ultimate destiny: Kept ○ Gifted ○ Sold ○

Cost to make me: __________

If gifted or sold, person received: ______________________________

If sold, price and date: ______________________________

Additional notes:

Selfie

Date I was created: ______________________________

How tall I am: __________ My colors: ______________________

Theme or holiday: ______________________________

The name my human gave me: ______________________________

Materials Used to Make Me	Bought From	Price
Hat/hair:		
Body:		
Nose:		
Beard:		
Arms/legs:		
Shoes:		
Filling/stuffing:		
Other:		
Embellishments:		
Accessories:		

Difficulty level: Easy ① ② ③ ④ ⑤ Hard

Was I commissioned? Yes ○ No ○

My ultimate destiny: Kept ○ Gifted ○ Sold ○

Cost to make me: __________

If gifted or sold, person received: ______________________________

If sold, price and date: ______________________________

Additional notes: ________________________________

____

____

____

____

____

____

____

____

Selfie

Date I was created: ____________________

How tall I am: __________ My colors: ____________________

Theme or holiday: ____________________

The name my human gave me: ____________________

Materials Used to Make Me	Bought From	Price
Hat/hair:		
Body:		
Nose:		
Beard:		
Arms/legs:		
Shoes:		
Filling/stuffing:		
Other:		
Embellishments:		
Accessories:		

Difficulty level: Easy ① ② ③ ④ ⑤ Hard

Was I commissioned? Yes ○ No ○

My ultimate destiny: Kept ○ Gifted ○ Sold ○

Cost to make me: __________

If gifted or sold, person received: ____________________

If sold, price and date: ____________________

Additional notes:

Selfie

Date I was created: ______________________________

How tall I am: __________ My colors: __________________

Theme or holiday: ______________________________

The name my human gave me: ______________________________

Materials Used to Make Me	Bought From	Price
Hat/hair:		
Body:		
Nose:		
Beard:		
Arms/legs:		
Shoes:		
Filling/stuffing:		
Other:		
Embellishments:		
Accessories:		

Difficulty level: Easy ① ② ③ ④ ⑤ Hard

Was I commissioned? Yes ○ No ○

My ultimate destiny: Kept ○ Gifted ○ Sold ○

Cost to make me: __________

If gifted or sold, person received: ______________________________

If sold, price and date: ______________________________

Additional notes:

Selfie

Date I was created: ______________________________

How tall I am: __________ My colors: ______________________

Theme or holiday: ______________________________

The name my human gave me: ______________________________

Materials Used to Make Me	Bought From	Price
Hat/hair:		
Body:		
Nose:		
Beard:		
Arms/legs:		
Shoes:		
Filling/stuffing:		
Other:		
Embellishments:		
Accessories:		

Difficulty level: Easy ① ② ③ ④ ⑤ Hard

Was I commissioned? Yes ○ No ○

My ultimate destiny: Kept ○ Gifted ○ Sold ○

Cost to make me: __________

If gifted or sold, person received: ______________________________

If sold, price and date: ______________________________

Additional notes:

Selfie

Date I was created: ____________________

How tall I am: __________ My colors: ____________________

Theme or holiday: ____________________

The name my human gave me: ____________________

Materials Used to Make Me	Bought From	Price
Hat/hair:		
Body:		
Nose:		
Beard:		
Arms/legs:		
Shoes:		
Filling/stuffing:		
Other:		
Embellishments:		
Accessories:		

Difficulty level: Easy ① ② ③ ④ ⑤ Hard

Was I commissioned? Yes ○ No ○

My ultimate destiny: Kept ○ Gifted ○ Sold ○

Cost to make me: __________

If gifted or sold, person received: ____________________

If sold, price and date: ____________________

Additional notes:

Selfie

Date I was created: ____________________

How tall I am: __________ My colors: ____________________

Theme or holiday: ____________________

The name my human gave me: ____________________

Materials Used to Make Me	Bought From	Price
Hat/hair:		
Body:		
Nose:		
Beard:		
Arms/legs:		
Shoes:		
Filling/stuffing:		
Other:		
Embellishments:		
Accessories:		

Difficulty level: Easy ① ② ③ ④ ⑤ Hard

Was I commissioned? Yes ○ No ○

My ultimate destiny: Kept ○ Gifted ○ Sold ○

Cost to make me: __________

If gifted or sold, person received: ____________________

If sold, price and date: ____________________

Quick Reference Index

Pages	Date	Project – Gnome's Name
1-2		
3-4		
5-6		
7-8		
9-10		
11-12		
13-14		
15-16		
17-18		
19-20		
21-22		
23-24		
25-26		
27-28		
29-30		
31-32		
33-34		
35-36		
37-38		
39-40		
41-42		
43-44		
45-46		
47-48		
49-50		

Quick Reference Index

Pages	Date	Project – Gnome's Name
51-52		
53-54		
55-56		
57-58		
59-60		
61-62		
63-64		
65-66		
67-68		
69-70		
71-72		
73-74		
75-76		
77-78		
79-80		
81-82		
83-84		
85-86		
87-88		
89-90		
91-92		
93-94		
95-96		
97-98		
99-100		

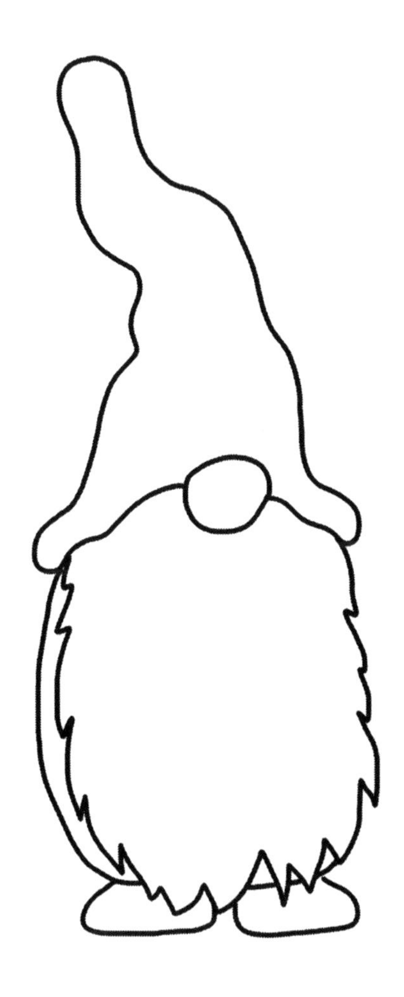

If you liked the book I made and you found it helpful to keep track of all the details that went into making more of my friends, you have gnome idea how much I would appreciate it if you left a review on Amazon for me.

If you are making more friends for me,
it's probably time to buy another gnome tracker book.

Thank you,

Ima Gnome

Made in United States
Orlando, FL
14 June 2023

34147923R00059